I0829872

I would like to acknowledge the valuable insights and support of the following individuals:

Emily Toder, Editor
Rafael Alfonso, Graphic Designer

ISBN: 9781793218070

Amazon's trademark is used under license from Amazon.com, Inc. or its affiliates.

DEMYSTIFYING
Corporate Branding

An Innovative Guide Rooted in Real-Life Examples

Jose Ignacio Monrabal

Dedicated to:

Lorena, for *being* my light
My father, for *mentoring* me
My mother, for *understanding* me
Benja, for *influencing* me
Javier, for *vitalizing* me
Rafa, for *inspiring* me

Thank you for always supporting me.

When it comes to communicating, brands and people are not all that different.

Both have an identity, a purpose in life, values, and motivations.

Both use visual and verbal cues to express their essence and their aspirations.

Both work hard to cultivate and maintain an image that accurately reflects their spirit and personality, to reflect no more and no less.

Both are invested in their reputation and how they are perceived by those around them.

RICOH
RICOH
CASIO
FOND
C'BON COSMETICS
Le Cafe Doutor
英会話＆留学
ジオス
鳩居堂

CONTENTS

#1

INTRODUCTION

WHY AN ANALOGY BETWEEN HUMAN BEINGS AND BRANDS?

THE AUTHOR'S MOTIVATIONS TO WRITE THIS BOOK

It's always surprised me how mysterious corporate branding can be to the general public. Most people have an oversimplified and somewhat inaccurate understanding of the tasks undertaken by corporate marketing and branding professionals. Some might think that serve the sole purpose of boosting sales, or that all it takes is a little work on brand image, advertising, or promotional campaigns. Sometimes, even the most skilled branding specialists have trouble describing the scope of their work clearly, and without relying on the industry's latest buzzwords, using clear language and cogent examples to make themselves fully understood.

Since the 1980's, when corporate branding began to receive more attention from the business world, many books and articles have been published on the subject. But despite the vast availability of information, and the growing number of experts in this field, I believe that the general public, and particularly those in other areas of business management, have yet to fully understand the nuances of the branding sector and the motives and values that drive most of the work conducted in its guise.

In my experience, when it comes to communicating, brands and people are not all that different. Both have identities, a purpose in life, values and motivations. Both use verbal and visual cues to express their values and their aspirations; both work hard to cultivate and maintain an image that accurately reflects their essence and personality; and both are invested in their reputation and how they are perceived by those around them.

While I'd worked in branding for a substantial amount of time, it wasn't until 2014 that I discovered a clear and simple way of explaining the scope of my job to family and friends. Before delving into technical details, I provided a streamlined introduction to the core concepts of corporate branding, and developed my own story to explain what branding is all about.

The approach, which I delivered and refined over the course of 20 workshops given around the world, explored simple analogies between brands and everyday life, by asking simple questions like: What is my purpose in life? How do I dress every day and why? What do I say everyday and why? How am I expressing myself?, and how am I perceived? From there, I could explain how these same questions function, and can be answered, when it comes to brands.

This book is not about personal branding. Instead, it sets out to explore how the fundamental aspects of corporate branding can be simply understood by drawing connections between personal expression and corporate communications.

I believe that in order to like something, one has to first understand it. I hope this book helps you to better understand corporate brands and how they are managed, and that you become as passionate about the art and science of branding as I am.

WHAT MAKES THIS BOOK DIFFERENT FROM OTHER BOOKS?

CORE LEARNING OBJECTIVES AND SCOPE

This book is not intended to help the reader to master the practice of corporate branding. There are actually many good books that already exist on the subject, and in any case, such a study calls for many more pages, as well as technical and complex language.

This book adopts a different approach to the subject. While its scope might seem very ambitious, given the plethora of information available today, this book is designed to clearly explain the core concepts of branding using everyday language, examples, and experience. Therefore it is perfect for those who want to gain an understanding of the world of corporate branding without getting lost in the complexities of its strategic implementation or convoluted terminology.

Because this book focuses on the concepts that underlie corporate branding, and not its actual management, it does not address some of the more technical and executional principles related to the daily governance of a corporate brand.

This book could be, or should be, the very first book you read about branding. But it probably won't be the last. And, if it stirs a deep interest in you, and you find yourself growing passionate about branding, there is a lot more reading in store for you!

WHO IS THIS BOOK INTENDED FOR?
INTENDED AUDIENCE

This book is primarily intended for students and junior professionals in the fields of corporate brand management, communications, marketing, advertising, design, sales, and eventually human resources and corporate strategy.

This book will walk you through the core concepts behind the discipline of corporate branding. As you peruse this guide, you will become familiar with the essential principles of the field, and gain a basic but thorough understanding of its core components.

But beginners are not the only ones who stand to benefit from reading this book. Senior administrators or corporate branding professionals will enjoy exploring familiar terrain from a wholly new perspective. Those already well-versed in the field will also learn a simple and direct way of explaining their practice to others, including students interested in pursuing studies in branding, or in-house trainees who are just starting in the arena.

Last but not least, this book can provide a swift but cogent overview of the core concepts behind corporate branding, perfect for experienced professionals specializing in other areas of business management, such as corporate strategy or human resources.

#2

UNDERSTANDING CORPORATE BRANDING

AN ANALOGY BETWEEN HUMAN BEINGS AND BRANDS

WHO ARE WE?
BRAND VALUES AND PURPOSE

Each morning we follow certain principles in the simple act of getting dressed. We might adorn our bodies with all sorts of decorative elements, but still, we adhere to certain criteria. We put on clothing and add accessories and other aesthetic elements as we stand before the mirror. Some elements are functional, like watches or scarves, while others serve purely aesthetic purposes, like bracelets. While to a certain degree, we dress in accordance with the general standards or expectations of society, in another sense, we adjust or customize our look to best reflect our personality, our values, and our purpose in life. It's our identity or self-concept which brings us to choose one shirt over another, pick a particular tie, or don a certain hairstyle.

Later, when we strike up our first conversation of the day, independently of these means of expression, we reflect, directly or indirectly, who we are, what we aspire to, and what we believe.

Our identity develops over the course of our experience. It may be informed by things we've been taught, feats we've accomplished, or goals we set out to achieve. Our lives may be guided by a sense of purpose, upon which we base our ethical, religious, or other grounding beliefs. And these values are expressed steadily, however subtly, in everything we do.

Just like people, brands need to express themselves in order to stay true to their beliefs, and to express their future goals and past accomplishments.

Wally Olins, former Chairman of Saffron Brand Consultants and Co-Founder of Wally Olins, defined branding as "a profound manifestation of the human condition. It is about belonging: belonging to a tribe, to a religion, to a family. Branding demonstrates that sense of belonging."

Like people, companies have a past, present, and future. Their history, current situation, and long-term ambitions are driven fundamentally by their values, and their purpose.

This brand purpose, is grounded on our values and aspirations. It has a healthy mix of factual past accomplishments and future goals. That gap in between is important, it defines the rest of the journey, it defines the direction to follow in everything we do.

For individuals and corporate entities alike, values and purpose form the basis of identity. This connection ensures that we remain unique to ourselves. And as we will see later, in the case of corporate brands, differentation is a key-driver of success.

HOW DO WE DRESS?
BRAND AWARENESS AND VISUAL EXPRESSION

Each morning, we wash up, get dressed, and get ourselves ready for the day. We decide how we want to be seen by the world when we step out onto the street. While there are many aspects of our appearance that cannot be modified, we do enjoy a certain degree of control over our external visual perception.

For a company, the very act of being seen is called "visual exposure." Although other factors may play a key role, visual exposure makes it possible for people to be aware that the brand exists; this is what's known as "brand awareness." When we're in public, we are going to be seen, whether we like it or not – but we can affect our appearance and cultivate a unique look that we think reflects us.

The same may be said of companies. Their presence is expressed through each of the brand's visual touch-points with the market, such as mass emails, website features, and signage.

The visual communication serves as the starting point for how corporations wish to be seen. Visual expression is not the origin of our identity, but rather an expression thereof. Both brands and people use visual cues to express themselves and convey their value systems. And these visual aspects play a huge role, because they are, in the end, what the world sees.

WHAT DO WE SAY?
BRAND VERBAL EXPRESSION

A picture may say a thousand words, but words are still quite important. Every day we exchange words with the people around us, be they family members in the kitchen, strangers on the street, coworkers in the office, or friends at the bar. Moreover, the words we use are not only heard; they may be read as well, whenever we write an email or leave a note on the fridge. The words we use, both spoken and written, may be called our "verbal expression."

You might be very well put together and elegantly dressed. But it won't take you very far if you only utter outlandish and nonsensical things every time you open your mouth. In just the same way, companies may have an attractive image, but in the end, what they say counts for a lot. We don't judge people based purely on their appearance; while this informs part of our perspective, we also pay a lot of attention to the things people express in their own words. Verbal expression enables greater content and depth through clear, tangible, and precise language. That is part of what makes verbal communication so important.

Visual expression may be interpretable, but language itself is understood uniformly by all. This makes "verbal expression" of vital importance, for people and companies alike.

HOW DO WE SAY IT?
TONE OF VOICE

Sometimes what we say makes a lot of sense, but we express it poorly and are misunderstood as a result. Other times, the way in which we say something doesn't really suit its meaning, because of the mood we're in. We might say something essentially harmless in a tone that makes it sound harsh or tell an exciting story so blandly that it bores our listeners. The content of our message is controlled through our tone of voice; how we say what we say. The reception of our message is founded not only on the words we choose, but the style, tone, and body language we use as we say them.

For companies, tone of voice is no less important. How we say something is often just as crucial as what we say.

Tone of voice is crucial in corporate communications; it can color the content and meaning of their message, and reflect effectively the essence of their identity and purpose.

WHY DO WE DRESS HOW WE DRESS? WHY DO WE SAY WHAT WE SAY?

BRAND CONSISTENCY

Our identity is defined on the basis of coherence. How would our colleagues see us if one day we randomly show up at the office in all sorts of different garb? What would our friends think if every day we had a totally different things to say, from one day to the next?

Dressing each day in a steady, reasonably consistent style, and saying things that reflect a steady value system or personality make our identity coherent. In the business world, this phenomenon is called "brand consistency." Looking nice on a random day is not enough; in order to be perceived as dressing well, one has to dress well on a regular basis. To inspire trust, and to make yourself truly known and understood overtime, you need to have some consistency in your outward appearance, and in your verbal cues and content.

Although visual expression may be simpler to interpret (and is certainly easier to see), inconsistencies may be spotted in both visual and verbal communications. In the life of an individual, or that of a corporate brand, looking and sounding reasonably consistent day-to-day is hugely important. Each time in which we break with our routine expression or stray from how we normally present ourselves in the world, we may jeopardize the image we've cultivated over the course of months, or even years.

At the end of the day, our identity depends on the consistency with which it is expressed. After all, the merits of our identity can't be evaluated if our values are seen to vary from one day to the next. Identity simply crumbles if it isn't expressed in a solid and steady manner.

At the end of the day, branding is about building trust. And trust has to be earned. And an indispensable way of earning that trust is being consistent within yourself; being coherent, repeatedly. When people and brands are consistent in how they look and what they say, they allow others to really develop a clear understanding of who they are, and what they stand for. It is only on the basis of this solid understanding that a lasting and meaningful relationship may be built.

As Tony Robbins, an American motivational speaker, says, "It's not what we do once in a while that shapes our lives. It's what we do consistently."

The same is true of companies. To inspire the trust, interest, and loyalty of stakeholders, brands have to endeavor to make their identity, image, and message consistent on a day-to-day basis, and through each and every corporate communication or expression.

This goes for both verbal and visual communications. It is not enough just to be seen on a daily basis; brands need to be seen consistently, and cultivate messages that are aligned with their values and goals. If these aspects are seen to change from one day to the next, it is very difficult to inspire trust within the market. Brand awareness is indispensable to visibility and presence in the market, but it should always be accompanied accompanied by reputation, founded upon coherence and consistency. Just like individuals, corporate entities need to be known and understood in order to be fully trusted. And it's quite hard to trust a person or brand that seems to change at its core each time it expresses itself.

Despite how crucial consistency is, it is still generally much underestimated in the corporate world. After all, it can be very tempting to switch up the routine, particularly after a company has been using the same means of expression for years on end. Of course, there are times at which changes are necessary; but still, any genuine change is carried out gradually, and with great thought and care. A communications department should not endeavor to make great modifications just for the sake of switching things up; instead, it should employ changes to evolve its identity, amplify the brand's expression, or make communications more effective. In that sense, making small changes from time to time might actually be necessarily to remain updated, so long as each change is given careful consideration and works to truly and clearly manifest the identity of the brand.

HOW CAN WE BE SURE WE'RE BEING CONSISTENT ENOUGH?
CORPORATE BRAND GUIDELINES

Larger companies, with thousands of employees and multiple channels of communication with the outside world, usually end up needing a code; a manual that ensures a consistent brand voice across the hundreds of communications produced every day by thousands of people with different personality types and from all around the world.

We refer to this "code" as "brand guidelines," and by following them closely, companies can ensure that their thousands of employees and agencies communicate with the outside world in a consistent fashion which reflects a single and unique personality, based on core values and purpose: those which ground the company identity.

In our personal lives, the guidelines that we follow are usually not formally scripted documents; they live instead in our hearts, minds, and instincts. It's easy enough to keep these in our heads, since after all, we're the only ones using them! However, in the case of a company, it is not one mind or heart that expresses an identity; it may be as many as thousands of employees. And therefore, corporate guidelines need to be not only written down and formally recorded, but consulted each and every day.

WHEN AND WHERE DO WE SAY WHAT WE SAY?
MARKETING CHANNELS

Context plays a huge role in how we express ourselves. Sometimes an idea we have may be really interesting or accurate, but it's not the right time to share it. Or we may find that certain notions are inappropriate to share in certain company. Just like in the physical world, in the communications realm, space and time are fundamental axes. The questions of "where" and "when" can be central to the "what" of our message. And just like the other aspects we've examined thus far – visual expression, verbal expression, and tone of voice – choosing the right place and time is absolutely essential to getting the message across in the most effective way.

With experience, people are usually able to manage this technique better and better as they grow older. And companies can improve with time, too. According to the 4Ps Marketing Mix model by McCarthy, one of the key components of the "Promotion" phase is identifying the time and place within the market to send a message. This is the same technique ordinary people have been following forever in their personal lives.

In branding, the "where" or "when" isn't the whole story, but it plays a fundamental role. Using the proper channels to reach a certain audience is absolutely key to being heard and understood in the way we intend.

WHAT IS IT LIKE TO DEAL WITH US?

BRAND EXPERIENCE

People might care a great deal about who we are, and how we express ourselves. But even more important is the experience they have when they're around us – how much they enjoy our company, what they feel, what they are able to learn… essentially, how positive their experience is.

Every individual is unique; and, as we saw earlier, uniqueness and identity are jeopardized in the absence of consistency. In the same way, the perception of an identity can be weakened if the actual experience of that identity is unpleasant. Even when we agree with a certain individual's ideas, we may have trouble enjoying his or her company, if those ideas are expressed in a hostile or otherwise unpleasant way. The same thing happens in business:

Experience is in many ways the bottom line. A customer might not have such fondness for our noble messages or concern for our refined beliefs if what they receive is a defective product or a negative service experience. So on an operational level, brands have to care not only about how they express their values, but also how they manage consumer expectations, how they monitor service and product quality, and how they ensure their customers and stakeholders a positive and rewarding experience throughout each and every interaction. We also call this the "customer experience," and what we deliver through our products, services and relationships, is actually what drives the perceptions of our brand, not what we communicate.

HOW DO OTHERS PERCEIVE US?

BRAND REPUTATION

As soon as people spend time with us, they begin to form a perception of who we are. Ideally, this perception is not far off the identity we seek to put forward. But sometimes people don't see us for who we truly are – and our identity does not come across clearly. Just like people, companies can be judged harshly based on how they present themselves to the world. And sometimes these perceptions are not all that evident to us. As Jeff Bezos, founder of Amazon, says, "Your brand is what people say about you when you're not in the room."

A person's ability to express his or her identity through outward expression is crucial, because it will have an immediate impact on how that person is perceived. If core values are omitted or misrepresented in a person's verbal or visual communications, that person may be completely misunderstood. That's why it's so important that communications be well formed and carefully considered.

We have already explored how visual and verbal communication is central to expressing ourselves publicly, and how tone of voice and consistency play a huge role in conveying our true selves. All of these aspects should be used not to construct or falsely enhance our identity; rather, they should work to ensure that our identity is accurately conveyed and understood.

We all know that people have reputations, which form over the course of time. Companies, too, have reputations. And corporate reputations are just as central to a company's success and growth as it may be to an individual's well-being in a social context.

Indeed, in the corporate world, reputation is even more important, since often times a company's perception has a greater and more lasting impact than that company's actual beliefs or identity.

In the 1980s, these notions began to be referred to as "corporate identity" and "corporate image." The job of the communications team, and particularly its branding experts, is not to make the image bigger or better than the identity, but rather to make it a true reflection thereof. In this regard, we may use the terms "corporate reputation" and "corporate image" interchangeably.

Reputation can be a driver of success, or it can lead straight to bankruptcy – particularly in a market as competitive as today's. And in a world so constantly plugged in to the internet and social networks, perception has the power to influence many people, and therefore make a truly exponential impact, for good or for ill.

HOW ARE WE VALUED?

BRAND PREFERENCE

Reputation and perception can mean a great deal in personal relationships. But in the end, what really matters is that the people who know us value us and cherish us dearly.

For brands, this translates into customer loyalty. A brand may be well perceived and its values may be respected, but in the end, what really matters is that its customers favor it over all its competitors. And in addition to the quality of our products or services, the choices customers make are driven in a significant manner by what we call "brand preference."

Surprisingly, reputation and brand preference are not always closely linked. We might have a lot of admiration for a certain friend, but in practice, when things get tough, we might actually call on someone else for help when we need it most. The same thing happens in business.

Philip J. Duncan, the Global Design Officer of P&G, writes: "A brand is something you have an unexplained, emotional connection to. A brand gives you a sense of familiarity."

In our personal lives, this favorability manifests in social engagements and group activities. In the business world, it's more about finding opportunities to build loyalty, which means facilitating product sales on a regular basis.

HOW DO WE MANAGE OURSELVES?
BRAND MANAGEMENT

In our personal lives, the things that affect our external reputation are not relayed with formal communications. More often, managing the way we are perceived is directly related to how we manage ourselves in social situations.

In the business world, managing brand image for specialized resources and talents that not all companies – large or small – necessarily possess. This may involve things like graphic design, as well as verbal communication, strategy and operational skills. And managing all of these elements is by no means simple.

This is what's known as the art of "brand management" – basically, being able to manage and internally drive all the brand efforts to communicate effectively with the outside world.

As Brian Resnick and Carlos Martínez Onaindía stated in the book 'Designing B2B Brands, Lessons from Deloitte and 195,000 brand managers' (Wiley, 2013), "It takes several months to create a multifaceted system of brand elements and applications, but it requires years of strategic implementation and activation to achieve market penetration and recognition. The management of all brand assets is no less important than the asset themselves."

WHAT ARE OUR RIGHTS?
COPYRIGHTS AND TRADEMARKS

Most people enjoy certain inalienable rights; generally, the right to freedom, to express one's own identity, to be who one is.

The corporate world also guarantees certain rights: namely copyright, which protects creative work. But if we're talking about protection of brands themselves, the more poignant right is that which is protected by registered trademarks.

The world would be a very different place if others could legally steal our names, assume our identities, and carry out actions unauthorized on our behalf.

The same could be said of the business world. If the world's top brands could be used by others, for commercial purposes – if others were allowed to borrow the brand name, and lift the logo, the world might be a very unfair and chaotic place. And ultimately, we would not be able to really differentiate products and services from others, and this means we would not be able to make real choices.

The intellectual property laws and regulations surrounding trademarks establish a framework that grants corporate identities certain minimum rights; and which allow corporate entities to cultivate and maintain a unique identity.

COMPARISON FROM A COMMUNICATIONS STANDPOINT

THE CORPORATE BRAND

Stands for its employees, its strategy, its code of ethics, its values...

Has a purpose, like providing quality products, making the world a better place, creating jobs...

Is seen on its website, social networks, meetings, trade shows, magazines...

Speaks to employees, candidates, customers, suppliers, investors, the media, the community...

Writes emails, websites, blogs, reports, brochures, magazines...

Inspires employees, customers, suppliers, followers, the community...

Spends time designing things, developing guidelines, managing brand assets, engaging, training...

Has a Corporate Reputation

THE INDIVIDUAL BRAND

Stands for its family values, ethical code, religious values, personal beliefs...

Has a purpose in life, like raising a family, being happy, being a good person...

Is seen at home, at work, on the street, on the bus, in the mall...

Speaks to family members, coworkers, friends, shopping and service agents...

Writes emails, Facebook messages, blog posts, texts, WhatsApp messages...

Inspires family members, coworkers, friends...

Spends time developing personally, pursuing interests, learning new things...

Has a Personal Reputation

#3

ANALYSIS

UNDERSTANDING CORPORATE BRANDS
THROUGH EVERYDAY REALITIES

EVERYDAY ANALOGIES FROM A COMMUNICATIONS STANDPOINT:
THE LIFE CYCLE OF THE BRAND

If we understand brands as intangible assets that come with their own values and communicate with the outside world, they really are not all that different from people. Both are born to develop their values and reach their goals, refine their identity, and express it to others.

The effectiveness with which both people and brands communicate with their audiences will depend in large part on their ability to express their values visually and verbally, in a suitable tone, and in a consistent basis. Only with these tools and abilities they can develop lasting and meaningful relationships with others.

The graphic in the next page shows much more simply the many similarities between people and corporate brands over the course of their lifetimes.

THE LIFE CYCLE OF THE BRAND'S IDENTITY

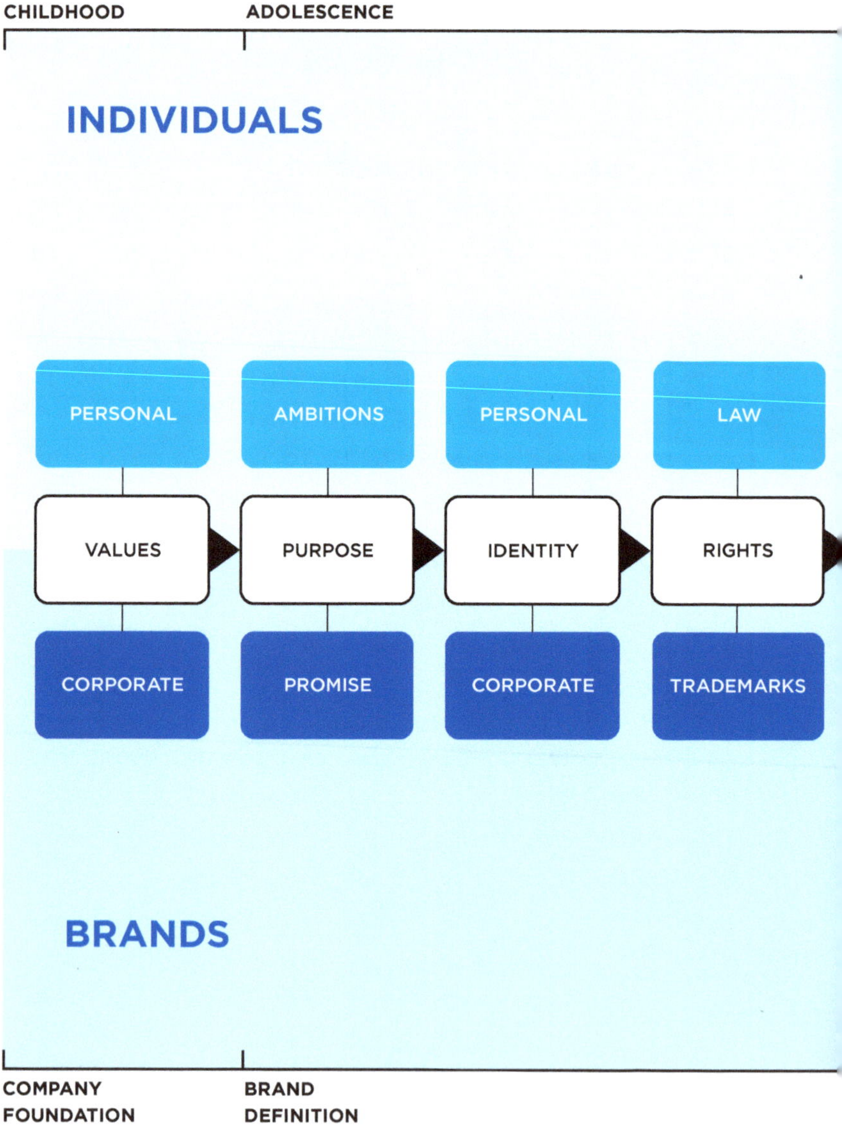

CHILDHOOD

ADOLESCENCE

INDIVIDUALS

PERSONAL	AMBITIONS	PERSONAL	LAW
VALUES	PURPOSE	IDENTITY	RIGHTS
CORPORATE	PROMISE	CORPORATE	TRADEMARKS

BRANDS

COMPANY
FOUNDATION

BRAND
DEFINITION

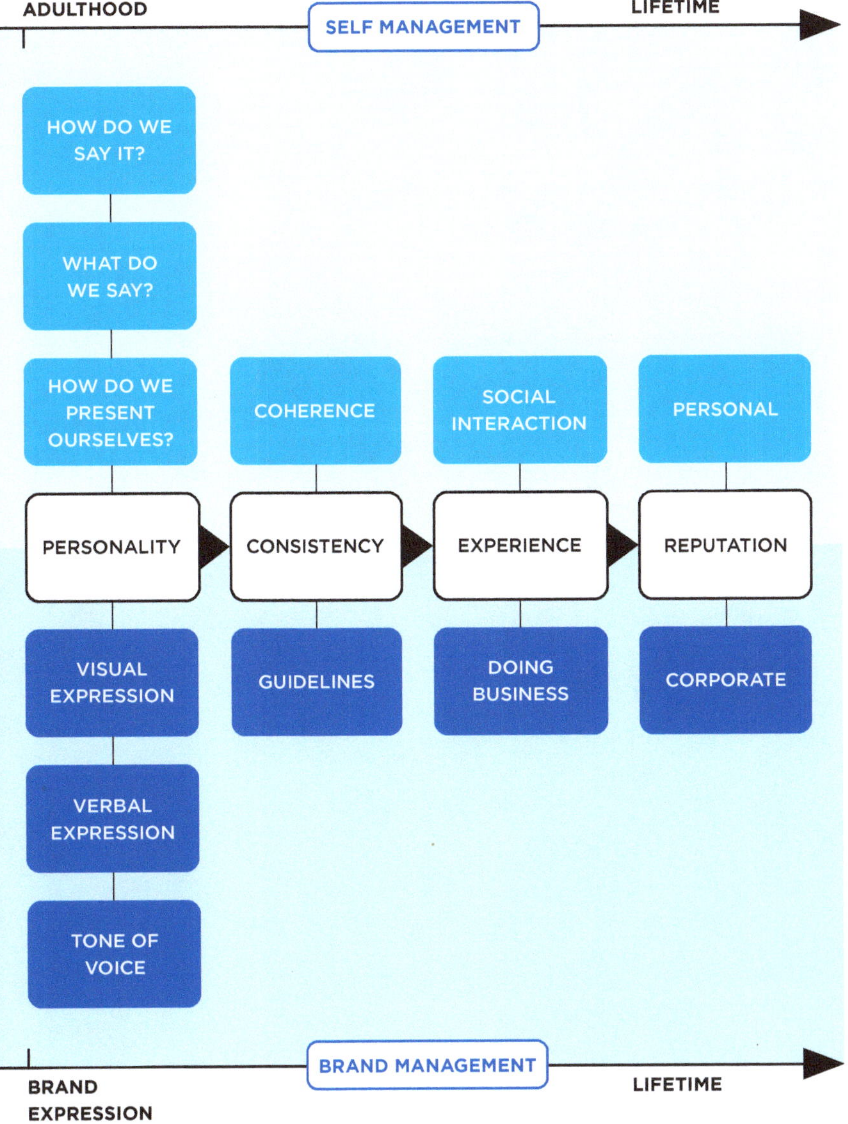
ADULTHOOD
SELF MANAGEMENT
LIFETIME
HOW DO WE SAY IT?
WHAT DO WE SAY?
HOW DO WE PRESENT OURSELVES?
COHERENCE
SOCIAL INTERACTION
PERSONAL
PERSONALITY
CONSISTENCY
EXPERIENCE
REPUTATION
VISUAL EXPRESSION
GUIDELINES
DOING BUSINESS
CORPORATE
VERBAL EXPRESSION
TONE OF VOICE
BRAND MANAGEMENT
LIFETIME
BRAND EXPRESSION

STANDING OUT FROM THE CROWD
CREATIVITY IN COMMUNICATIONS

While our personality is rooted in values and aspirations, we sometimes try to accentuate our personality, or attempt to alter its perception, by using creative means to stand out from the crowd. It could be through a different hairstyle, a flashy car, a particular way of dressing, or even a manner of dancing, that we show a unique side of ourselves, and manifest a desire for this side to be readily observed by those around us.

But sometimes this exaggerated expression of identity actually works to obscure our true nature, instead of shining a light on it. At what point does it stop being a natural reflection of personal identity, and instead become an obvious extravagance clearly adopted to attract attention or simply for the fact of standing out?

The temptation to overdo it happens even more often in the business world, where the need to compete is obviously greater than in a purely social environment. The competition in the corporate world is real and tough, and a company's success is subjectively but inevitably tied to the corporation's reputation. Still, sometimes within the professional context, one is tempted to use creativity as an end instead of a means. The idea might be: "let's do this because it's creative," instead of something along the lines of, "how am I going to do this? I am going to need creativity."

In this sense, we can't forget that just like people, a brand's final objective is to generate trust in others, built on the image they have cultivated, through coherence, and consistency. There are no shortcuts on the road to reputation; it's key to understand that a brand is built over the course of years, even decades.

When we get dressed each day, we don't put on the most inventive outfit that indulges the furthest depths of our creativity; instead, we base our choices first on what is practical (in terms of comfort and climate conditions), and then on what suits our individual personality. Finally, in the finishing details like our watch, tie, bracelet, necklace, or the color of our sweater, we allow ourselves to access our creativity in order to accentuate our personality. Still, this component should never contradict our core identity. It should complement it, and enhance it. Creativity is thus at the service of our brand consistency – not the other way around.

WHY CORPORATE BRANDING IS SO IMPORTANT FOR BUSINESS

THE VALUE OF REPUTATION

Each day, when we wake up and get ready for day, when we go out and interact with others, we are reflecting and communicating our personal identity. Our success as individual transmittors of whatever our message is has an identifying mark: that of our core being. The extent to which this personal essence is perceived properly by those around us depends on our communication skills and on our ability to reflect our values and aspirations in our daily behavior and outward appearance.

Branding professionals do something very similar each day when they arrive at the office. They remind themselves of the values and aspirations of the brand they work for. They express it visually in their communications; they add a verbal message in a tone that suits their brand identity and meets their communications objectives. Within this framework, and through corporate policies, brand guidelines, and information and training sessions, the brand endeavors to steadily communicate its story with the same basic shape and crux. Brands do this on an ongoing basis, until stakeholders take notice. Finally, they create an experience of that process, which is priceless in marketing. This experience which our stakeholders are able to perceive forms the basis of our "reputation."

As Robert Jones, Professor of Brand Leadership at the University of East Anglia, says in *The Secret Power of Brands*, "brands are the set of ideas a company or product stands for in people's minds, shaped by that company's or product's actions, and recognized through a visual and verbal style."

Now, if we replace "company or product" with "the individual," we can perfectly understand the strong analogy between corporate brands and people. What people stand for, the experience they deliver, and how they express themselves visually and verbally, is what determines value, loyalty, and lasting relationships, for both people and brands alike.

PERCEPTIONS THAT INVITE SELF-IMPROVEMENT

REPUTATION MANAGEMENT

Reputation is not only an end; it's also a means. Has a friend or family member ever told you that you weren't doing the greatest job at something? This one way in which it can be helpful to know how you are being perceived. Constructive criticism is likely to help you improve. The goal isn't perfection, but rather personal growth. Getting meaningful feedback from others can indeed help us better ourselves. And the same can be said in business.

Reputation has a retroactive function. By monitoring and paying attention to external agents, we can learn to correct our flaws. We can even use this feedback to make ourselves stand out from our competitors or other specific companies we admire.

Today it's rather easy to measure and evaluate our reputation. Through research, we can ask people how they feel about our brand in relation to our competitors. But learning is only half the battle; the real work is using this knowledge to actively and constantly improve. This effort is called "reputation management."

Just as in our personal lives, there are two critical requirements for managing corporate reputation successfully: intelligence and a flexible attitude. A person with a genuine appreciation for getting honest feedback, will incorporate criticism and use it as a starting point for implementing some changes. Brands are not different, they use any valuable feedback they get and use it to enhance their performance.

PRACTICING CORPORATE BRANDING

ETHICAL PRINCIPLES

Despite popular notion, ethics is also something branding professionals pay a great deal of attention to. Those working in branding fields don't regress to a Machiavellian mentality just to earn more money or sell an image that has no bearing on our product or service. On the contrary, branding professionals communicate and express their brands fairly and honestly, by trying to balance image with reality, and to transmit no more and no less.

Like our personal image, corporate image must be maintained continuously, each and every day. If we fail to keep it up, we appear messy and careless, qualities which are very easy to perceive. Working for a brand means taking care of it steadily, on a regular basis; and in a way that is honest and straightforward. It means, proudly reflecting the corporate strengths and business achievements we have arrived at.

Working in branding is very challenging, and requires professionals to balance the brand's need to promote itself with the carefully cultivated image it hopes to project, in order to maintain sales and foment the relationships it has crafted. Corporate branding is a complex and multifaceted exercise full of nuance.

Our values, together with the rigor with which we practice these principles, and our ability to accurately reflect who we are to the world, are the principal factors that can help our stakeholders better understand what our corporate brands stand for. The perception build out of these practices, will be key to conform a solid and lasting reputation.

Building a reputation for either corporations or individuals requires generating trust. And in the long-term, the only way to build trust is by being honest.

#4

STARTING A CAREER IN CORPORATE BRANDING

CORPORATE BRAND MANAGEMENT
DISCIPLINES

STARTING A CAREER IN CORPORATE BRANDING

CORPORATE BRAND MANAGEMENT DISCIPLINES

I hope that you've found this guide useful so far, and that it's helped you form a more nuanced understanding of what corporate brands do and how they're managed.

If you are interested in a new career in corporate brand management, you might want to consider pursuing studies in one or more of the following disciplines.

While there are not many dedicated programs in the world that focus on corporate brand management, most of the relevant skills can be learned on the job and there are also several dedicated courses on specific disciplines that later can help you build a solid background in this field.

On the following page you will find a summary of the various management, disciplines that touch on aspects of corporate branding.

Field of Expertise	Discipline	Typical Academic Background
Brand Management	·Brand Strategy ·Brand Management	·Corporate Branding ·Marketing ·Business Administration
Brand Development	·Identity Development ·Brand Purpose ·Brand Architecture ·Policies and Guidelines ·Naming ·Affiliate and M&A Branding	·Corporate Branding ·Creativity ·Graphic Design ·Copywriting ·Intellectual Property
Brand Activation	·Brand Communications ·Brand Experience ·Customer Experience ·Brand Culture	·Corporate Branding ·Sales & Marketing ·Business Administration
Marketing Communications (Marcom) and Advertising	·Advertising ·Marketing ·Communications ·Content Management ·Media Planning ·Creative Copywriting ·Co-Branding Communications ·Brand Sponsorships	·Advertising ·Marketing Communications ·Mass Communications ·Media and PR ·Journalism ·Marketing ·Sponsorships Management
Corporate Design, Photography and Video	·Graphic Design ·Assets Management ·Corporate Photography ·Video Production	·Graphic Design ·Fine Arts ·Photography ·Audiovisual Production
Reputation Management	·Reputation Monitoring and Tracking ·Quantitative Research ·Qualitative Research	·Business Administration ·Brand Strategy ·Market Research ·Sociology ·Psychology

Brand Protection	·Copyright and Trademarks ·Licensing	·Intellectual Property ·Brand Management
Employer 'Branding'	·Employer 'Brand' Management ·HR Communications	·Corporate Branding ·Corporate Communications ·Human Resources
Digital Marketing	·Content Management ·Websites ·Social Media ·SEM/SEO ·Apps	·Digital Marketing ·Digital Technologies ·Interactive Design ·Communications ·IT
Events and Exhibitions	·Events & Exhibitions ·Experiential Marketing ·Facility Branding	·Events Management ·Marketing ·Interior Design

#5

ABOUT
THE AUTHOR

JOSE IGNACIO MONRABAL

Jose Ignacio Monrabal holds a Master's Degree in Marketing Management from ESIC Business & Marketing School and an EMBA from Esden Business School, from which he graduated with honors.

He has worked in corporate brand management and marketing communications for several B2B companies, such as Altim, OSRAM, Siemens Group, Gandinnovations (later acquired by Agfa), Polymer Char, and SABIC.

At SABIC, one of the world's most valuable brands, Monrabal served as Senior Manager and Head of Global Brand Management, steering the company's brand strategy, protection, identity expression and communications for six years.

He has published articles on corporate branding in various prestigious publications, among them Advertising Age, DirCom Magazine, Branding Magazine, Marketing+Ventas, On-Brand Magazine, Marketing News, brandchannel and the Marketing for Scientific and Research Organizations monograph.

Monrabal was born in Spain and raised in the Netherlands. Over the course of his career, he's worked in Valencia, Madrid, Maastricht, as well as Riyadh, Saudi Arabia. He currently resides in his hometown, Valencia.

✉ joseignacio.monrabal@gmail.com
in www.linkedin.com/in/jimonrabal

INDEX

9 781793 218070